T0267647

STRESS

ALEX NOVAK

ROSEN PUBLISHING

Published in 2024 by The Rosen Publishing Group, Inc.
2544 Clinton Street, Buffalo, NY 14224

Portions of this work were originally authored by Elissa Thompson and published as *Coping with Stress*. All new material in this edition was authored by Alex Novak.

Designer: Rachel Rising
Editor: Corona Brezina

Names: Novak, Alex.
Title: Stress / Alex Novak.
Description: New York : Rosen Publishing, 2024. |
Series: Coping | Includes glossary and index.
Identifiers: ISBN 9781499474275 (pbk.) | ISBN 9781499474282 (library bound) | ISBN 9781499474299 (ebook)
Subjects: LCSH: Stress in adolescence--Juvenile literature. | Stress management--Juvenile literature.
Classification: LCC BF724.3.S86 N69 2024 | DDC 155.9'042--dc23t

Some of the images in this book illustrate individuals who are models. The depictions do not imply actual situations or events.

Manufactured in the United States of America

CPSIA Compliance Information: Batch #CSRYA24. For further information, contact Rosen Publishing at 1-800-237-9932.

Find us on

CONTENTS

CHAPTER 1
UNDERSTANDING STRESS 4

CHAPTER 2
STRESS OVERLOAD 14

CHAPTER 3
SOURCES OF STRESS 24

CHAPTER 4
WHEN STRESS GETS OVERWHELMING 40

CHAPTER 5
MANAGING STRESS 48

CHAPTER 6
SEEKING HELP 58

GLOSSARY 68
FOR MORE INFORMATION 70
FOR FURTHER READING 74
INDEX 76
ABOUT THE AUTHOR 80

UNDERSTANDING STRESS

Teenagers today are overloaded with stress. Many teens maintain grueling schedules of schoolwork and extracurricular activities. They feel under pressure to overachieve in order to be accepted into highly ranked colleges. That's on top of normal adolescent stress of maturing and establishing their own identities, not to mention the modern stressors such as social issues and climate change.

When stress becomes chronic, it can have serious consequences for physical and mental health. Stress can cause teenagers to feel anxious and overwhelmed. A stressed teenager may have trouble sleeping or focusing, which can affect their work and make them feel even more pressured. Fortunately, there are coping mechanisms that can help teens manage stress and adjust their perspective on the sources of unavoidable stress in their lives.

THE DISCOVERY OF STRESS

The word "stress" was coined when Hans Selye and another physician, Walter Bradford Cannon, began to publish the results of their research efforts back in the 20th century.

In his autobiography, *The Way of an Investigator*, Dr. Cannon theorized that when presented with severe stress, the body shuts down certain functions, like digestion, which aren't needed in life-or-death situations. By doing this, blood can move to parts of the body, including the brain, heart, lungs, and muscles, where it is needed immediately. Thus, the concept of the fight-or-flight response was born.

Dr. Hans Selye, known as "the father of stress research," was a highly respected endocrinologist—a doctor specializing in the body's hormones.

Dr. Selye differentiated between good and bad stress. Good stress, which he called eustress, is comprised of bodily responses to stressors that help protect one in times of danger. Bad stress, which he called distress, is an excess of stress. Stress responses are automatic, and one can't do anything to stop them from occurring. If a person is constantly being stressed, their body's stress reactions will begin to overlap. Temporary bodily changes, like elevated blood pressure and heart rate, may become present all the time.

When the body is under a state of constant stress, it can contribute to the development of significant health problems, including heart attacks and strokes.

The human body responds to sources of stress when under threat, triggered by a rush of hormones that affects various physical systems.

STRESS AND THE BODY

It's impossible to go through an entire day without encountering stressors and reacting to them. Regardless of what the stressor is, the body will react the same way every time it is stressed. Here's what happens:

Heart rate, respiratory rate, and blood pressure increase. At the same time, blood flow to the skin, digestive system, and kidneys decreases. As a result, more blood is shunted to organs, like the lungs, brain, and large muscle groups, which really need it in emergency situations. When blood flow is increased to the brain, its ability to respond quickly to stressors improves. Increased blood flow to large muscle groups enables one to flee from a perceived danger.

Sweating increases. The chemical reactions occurring in the body in response to stress create a lot of body heat. Increased sweating helps the body eliminate this extra heat.

The pupils dilate, or enlarge. When the pupils dilate, they allow more light into the eyes to improve vision.

Stored glycogen is released from the liver. When undergoing a stress reaction, the body needs a lot of extra energy to fuel its systems. The body's energy source is glucose, a form of sugar. The liver, which stores sugar as glycogen, releases it in response to stress.

Stored platelets and clotting factors release. If one gets a cut on their finger, platelets, or small particles that circulate in the bloodstream, cause a chemical reaction that makes blood clot at the site of the cut. In a stress reaction, large numbers of platelets, which are stored in bone marrow, are sent out into the circulating blood. At the same time, chemicals called clotting factors, which are also necessary for blood clotting, are moved out of storage into the bloodstream to speed up the clotting mechanism if it is needed.

STRESS REACTIONS

When stressed, a series of reactions are kicked off within the body. Let's say you step off the curb onto the street while distracted, not noticing an oncoming car. Here is what happens:

The screech of the brakes travels to your ears, where it causes your eardrums to vibrate. The three bones of the middle ear carry those vibrations to nerve cells in your inner ears. There, they are converted to electrical impulses. From there, your auditory nerves carry these impulses to your brain.

The impulses travel deep into the brain to the hypothalamus. Here, cells begin to make a hormone called corticotropin-releasing hormone (CRH).

CRH is dumped into the blood and carried through small veins to your pituitary gland. Once CRH reaches the pituitary gland, it acts on the gland's cells and causes them to make another hormone called adrenocorticotropic hormone (ACTH).

A car is speeding toward you as you step into a crosswalk. Your body's stress reaction is activated, enabling you to respond quickly and retreat back onto the sidewalk.

ACTH is absorbed into the blood and carried all the way from the head to the adrenal glands, two clumps of tissue located just above the kidneys. There, ACTH causes cells of the adrenal glands to produce three hormones: cortisol, epinephrine, and norepinephrine.

The three hormones travel through the bloodstream to different places in your body. Cortisol goes to your liver, where it pushes glucose that is stored there into the blood. The glucose is then carried to organs that need it. Epinephrine and norepinephrine travel all over your body to stimulate your autonomic nervous system, which helps control the body during an emergency. Thanks to the epinephrine, your heart rate soars, and your blood pressure can shoot up too.

After you scramble back onto the curb unharmed, your stress reaction begins to subside. The reaction is turned off when you no longer need all the cortisol your adrenal glands are producing. The extra cortisol is carried back to the brain where it stops the hypothalamus from producing CRH. This is called a feedback mechanism, and it is one of the ways the body turns off reactions it no longer needs.

THE STAGES OF STRESS

Dr. Selye discovered that stress causes a three-stage pattern of response that he called the general adaptation syndrome (GAS), which is what happens to a body when it is stressed.

The Alarm Stage: When you stepped off the curb, you sensed a threat and your body responded to allow you to get back to the curb unharmed. After the car passed, your body's stress reaction was turned off and your physiologic parameters, like heart rate and blood pressure, started to return to normal.

The Adaptive/Resistance Stage: As you continue your walk down the street, you again hear screeching brakes. Although you are no longer in harm's way, you experience another stress reaction. However, your heart rate and blood pressure are not as high as with your first reaction.

The Exhaustion Stage: If you experience unrelenting stress, you may reach a point where you can no longer elicit a stress response.

Unrelenting stress is a big problem in the typical modern lifestyle. Stress isn't unhealthy if it's a temporary condition that subsides once the danger is past. But today, adults and teens alike feel constant stress to compete and achieve. And long-term stress can be damaging to both the body and the mind.

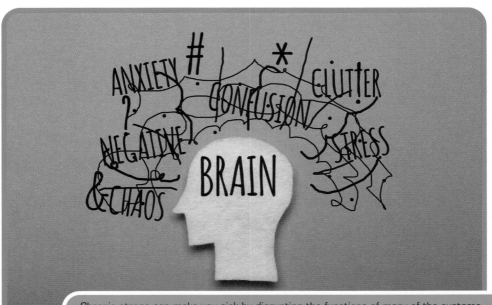

Chronic stress can make you sick by disrupting the functions of many of the systems of the body, affecting your thinking, emotions, behavior, and physical health.

MYTHS & FACTS

MYTH: Stress is always bad.

FACT: In some cases, stress can provide energy and motivation. The stress response can improve physical performance or energize you for a challenging project. When stress starts to impair your everyday functioning, however, you need to take steps to manage it.

MYTH: Everybody experiences stress the same way.

FACT: People all react differently to various sources of stress. Likewise, there's no single coping mechanism for dealing with stress that works for everybody. You'll have to try different approaches to find out what's effective for you.

MYTH: It's impossible to completely eliminate stress from my life, so there's no point in trying.

FACT: Stress management doesn't mean trying to cut out all sources of stress. But you can work to minimize the stressors in your life and take steps to control your response to stress so that you don't feel overwhelmed.

You might think that in today's high-pressure world, people have no choice but to live with the consequences of stress, but there are healthy ways to manage stress.

CHAPTER 2

STRESS OVERLOAD

Today, people can feel overwhelmed by near-constant sources of stress. Home life, school responsibilities, social media pressures, managing relationships, and handling major changes are a few possible causes of stress that might pile up on teens. Some people might feel so overloaded that they suffer from chronic stress, in which the body never has a chance to relax in between stressful experiences. A traumatic experience can also cause chronic stress. Chronic stress can be damaging to many systems of the body as well as to mental health.

STRESS AND THE BODY

Stress can hurt your physical health in a number of ways. You may not realize that when you've got a headache or nausea, stress could be a root cause.

STRESS AND IMMUNITY

The body's immune system is responsible for protecting it from foreign invaders such as bacteria or viruses. When the immune system kicks into gear, immune molecules coordinate an attack on foreign invaders.

Immune molecules can activate the hypothalamus, starting a typical stress reaction that results in the production of cortisol by the adrenal glands. Cortisol has the effect of making immune cells less effective in fighting invaders.

Overstressed people have consistently high levels of cortisol, and as a result, their immune systems are more susceptible to colds, the flu, or other infections.

Have you ever developed a fever blister or cold sore on your lip just before a big event like the prom? These lesions are symptoms of herpes simplex virus (HSV, which is a virus that can lie dormant in nerve tissue for years). Physical or emotional stress with immune system suppression is one of the most common causes of a new outcropping of blisters.

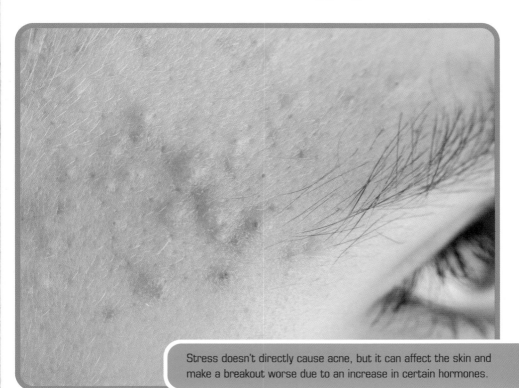

Stress doesn't directly cause acne, but it can affect the skin and make a breakout worse due to an increase in certain hormones.

GASTROINTESTINAL TROUBLE

Stomach aches before exams or a big game? Stress can also affect digestion and the gastrointestinal system.

A peptic ulcer is an area in the stomach or the first portion of the small intestine, the duodenum, where the normal lining of these organs, the mucosa, has been worn away. This hole in the mucosa allows the contents of the stomach, which contain a large amount of acid, to penetrate into the underlying muscles.

People with peptic ulcers have been shown to have large quantities of *H. pylori*, a common bacterium found in the human body, in their stomachs. *H. pylori* may multiply in the stomachs of these individuals because their immune systems cannot fight the bacteria off. As a result, they develop ulcers.

Many different factors contribute to people developing ulcers, including subjecting the body to stress, which can slow the healing process.

Irritable bowel syndrome (IBS) is what doctors call a "gut-brain interaction," and can cause abdominal pain, constipation, and diarrhea—or a mix of all three symptoms. Scientists at the National Institute of Diabetes and Digestive and Kidney Diseases believe IBS can be caused by food moving too slowly or quickly through your digestive system thanks to genetics, stress, or an infection.

HIGH BLOOD PRESSURE

Hypertension, or high blood pressure, is one of the main culprits in the development of atherosclerosis, a hardening of the arteries, which can lead to heart attacks and strokes. Epinephrine released in stress responses causes elevations in blood pressure and heart rate. In stress overload, large amounts of epinephrine are present in the circulatory system all the time. This causes very high blood pressure, especially in people who have inherited the tendency to develop hypertension.

According to the American Heart Association, about 103 million adults in the U.S. have high blood pressure—nearly half of the adult population.

WEIGHT

According to the Centers for Disease Control and Prevention (CDC), nearly one in five children from ages six to nineteen is obese, an amount that has tripled since the 1970s. Obesity is caused by many factors, including genetics and diet. Medical researchers are still working to find out how to combat obesity. But researchers do know that people who are stressed out produce large amounts of cortisol, and cortisol is known to increase appetite, which can cause weight gain.

OTHER CONCERNS

Extreme, long-term stress can cause other difficulties in the body as well. Here are two additional complications that can come from experiencing a lot of stress.

Reproductive malfunctions: Teens who are significantly stressed out have high amounts of cortisol circulating in their bloodstreams. In girls, this keeps ovaries from releasing eggs, and in boys, it keeps testes from releasing sperm. The production of testosterone, estrogen, and progesterone (sex hormones) is also impaired. Adult ballerinas and long-distance runners are examples of people who commonly have physical stress. These individuals, like teens with significant stress, are also known to have very high circulating cortisol levels.

Delayed growth: Children who are emotionally and physically abused at a young age can experience growth retardation. Their pituitary glands produce a lot of ACTH, adrenocorticotropic hormone, which produces cortisol in response to stress—at the expense of the production of growth hormone. If these children are placed in caring environments and receive sufficient positive attention, thereby reducing their stress levels, their growth will resume.

Some adult female athletes have reproductive problems related to the stress reaction that can last for several years after they stop training.

STRESS AND MENTAL HEALTH

Stress can also make people feel overwhelmed and affect their mental health. Stress is not itself a mental illness, but it can make other mental health conditions worse.

POST-TRAUMATIC STRESS DISORDER (PTSD)

People who experience traumatic stress can suffer severe mental health consequences as a result. Traumatic stress is caused when someone experiences or witnesses a dangerous or extremely disturbing event, such as a physical assault, a natural disaster, or a car accident. In the aftermath, they feel a rush of strong emotions such as fear, helplessness, and agitation. Normally, these fade with time. But for some people, intense emotions and symptoms persist long after the traumatic event. They may experience dreams or flashbacks related to the event. They may avoid people and places that remind them of the event and refuse to talk about it with others. They might have outbursts of strong emotions and difficulties in their personal relationships.

This mental health condition is called post-traumatic stress disorder (PTSD). It was first recognized as a psychiatric condition after being treated in war veterans who had experienced combat in battle, but it can occur following any type of traumatic event. PTSD may be accompanied by other issues, such as depression, substance abuse, and physical health problems.

PTSD can be a serious mental illness that requires treatment from a mental health professional. Talk therapy and medications such as antidepressants can help people recover from PTSD.

FEELINGS OF SADNESS AND SUICIDE

Some types of depression are characterized by anxiety, rapid heart rate, and high blood pressure, among other things. Do these signs sound familiar? These are the same signs found in stress reactions. In this disorder, the feedback mechanism for turning off CRH, the corticotropin-releasing hormone, does not work. Someone who develops depression when overstressed may do so because they are genetically programmed to produce too much CRH. In an apparent attempt to turn off CRH production, the body produces a lot of cortisol, but a side effect of having high levels of cortisol in your blood is depression.

Most teens who attempt suicide do so to escape from extremely stressful situations that seem impossible to deal with in any other way.

While not all types of depression are associated with high cortisol levels, depression is a frequent symptom seen in kids who are stressed out. When people feel that they can no longer cope with a stressful situation, they might think the only option is to escape from the situation by through suicide.

Not all suicides are planned. A suicide attempt is a call for help. Many teens have trouble telling their parents and friends how they feel. One may look at attempting suicide as a way of letting people know that they are hurting.

If you are experiencing significant depression and think there are no solutions to your problems, talk to someone about how you feel before your depression deepens to the point where you are unable to ask for help. If you feel like you can't talk with your parents, remember that hotlines are available in almost every community in the country, and there are also national toll-free numbers that you can call to get help. The key is to talk to someone. Tell an adult or call the National Suicide Prevention Lifeline at (800) 273-8255.

ANXIETY

Anxiety can be caused by the release of cortisol and adrenaline, hormones present when the body is stressed. Anxiety symptoms can also include racing heartbeat, hyperventilation, sleep problems, and more. Sometimes someone who has anxiety might even suffer a panic attack, a sudden feeling of intense fear when there is no real danger. If you have a panic attack, tell an adult and see a doctor for help right away.

According to WebMD, 43 percent of adults have health symptoms related to stress; 75 to 90 percent of visits to the doctor's office are related to stress. Teens are feeling the effects of stress, as well. According to a survey by the American Psychological Association, they're more stressed than adults, and they've been reporting higher levels of stress every year. Some people blame social media for this increase in stress. Others point to the urgent societal issues affecting the nation and world. When added to teens' everyday stresses, these factors can make modern adolescence even more challenging.

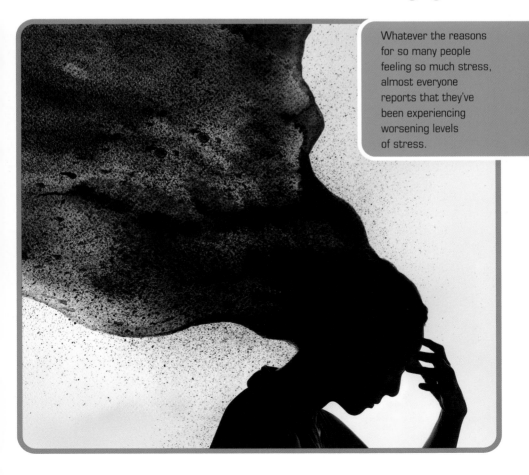

Whatever the reasons for so many people feeling so much stress, almost everyone reports that they've been experiencing worsening levels of stress.

CHAPTER 3

SOURCES OF STRESS

Being a teen has always been stressful, but today's teens face new pressures created by technology and societal issues. They're spending more and more of their time using social media, and they worry about climate change and school shootings and racial injustice. They're also dealing with the transition to adulthood, in which they're taking on more responsibilities and establishing their own identities. Many teens feel pressure to overachieve and fill their schedules with activities that will boost their chances of being accepted into a highly ranked college. For a teen, it might feel like the stress is piling up in every area of their life.

STRESSFUL FAMILY SITUATIONS

No family situation is stress-free. Even teens who are lucky enough to have caring parents and reasonable siblings are sometimes stressed by family issues. They know, however, that they can rely on family members for support. Some teens are not so lucky. The following stressors are among the hardest that teens deal with.

SEXUAL ABUSE

According to the CDC, one in four girls and one in thirteen boys in the United States are victims of sexual abuse. In over 90 percent of cases, the abuser is a family member or someone acquainted with the family.

Teens from abusive households may have been dealing with abuse for years. While one can adapt or cope, there will be scars—physical or emotional. Many of the coping mechanisms one might develop are negative ones. If you, a sibling, or a friend have been abused, tell a responsible adult. Talking to someone takes a great deal of courage, but it can be the only way to stop the abuse.

Sexual abuse is shockingly common, and it can cause significant stress and long-term mental health issues such as anxiety and depression.

DIVORCE

Divorce can be difficult for the entire family to handle. A teen might feel guilt over the divorce, concern about younger siblings, and worry regarding living situations. Perhaps your parents divorced when you were younger, or you are facing this extremely stressful situation now. Talking with an adult who is not directly involved—a school counselor, a teacher, or even the parent of a friend—may help you get through this difficult time.

ILLNESS AND DEATH

A major illness or the death of a parent or sibling is extremely stressful for a teen. Dealing with grief and wanting to be supportive for the remaining family members, all while coping with the other stresses of teen life, can be overwhelming. Teens may feel that they should be the supporters when all they really want to do is be supported. Remember that everyone grieves in their own way, in their own time. Talking about your feelings with a loved one can help.

Bereavement or coping with an illness among close family and friends can be a significant source of stress for teens.

Many teens feel stressed by the pressures of high school, from the everyday worries of maintaining grades to longer-term concerns such as college applications.

STRESSING OVER SCHOOL

School can be a stressful place, thanks to worries about grades, friends—and even safety. Getting into college, and concerns about expensive tuition, can also cause stress.

PARENTAL EXPECTATIONS

For many teens, living up to their parents' expectations can be extremely stressful. Most parents want their children to succeed, and school performance is one parameter that a parent looks at to judge whether a child is on the right track. However, a parent's definition of the "right track" can be quite different than their teen's.

Try talking with a teacher or school counselor who could give you advice on dealing with conflicts about parental expectations that don't match your own interests.

What do you do if your parents think you should pursue courses strong in the sciences, but your real interests and talents are in the arts? Conflicts like these are major stressors. They become even more significant if you can't talk to your parents about the problem or are unable to find a compromise that all of you can live with.

HOMEWORK OVERLOAD AND GRADES STRESS

The pressure to do well in school can be overwhelming. Teens stress out over their future plans and prospects for college. And then there's homework. The combination of school, homework, and extracurricular activities can lead to chronic stress for teens.

It can be stressful worrying about getting homework done. Remind yourself that one bad grade is not going to ruin your chances of having a nice life. If you're feeling overwhelmed by your schoolwork or discouraged by your grades, try talking to your teacher, school counselor, or parent.

It can be stressful worrying about getting the best grades to get into the best college to get the best job, but try to maintain some perspective.

ACTIVITY OVERLOAD

High school counselors often say that it takes more than grades for a teen to get into a good college or university. The question is: How much more? College admission committees check students' extracurricular activities to see if they've successfully held down jobs, done volunteer work, showed leadership skills in organizations, or developed athletic, artistic, or musical skills. These criteria give admission committee members a feel for what a student's interests are. Nonetheless, college admissions officers generally consider it impossible to measure or compare the quality of a student's extracurricular activities, so your chances of being admitted to a college are not necessarily enhanced by the number of extracurricular activities you report.

Some teens may be carrying the push to be "well-rounded" too far. Many are packing so much into their lives that they are truly stressed out. Teens are being overwhelmed by the demands on their time.

For some high schoolers, the demands of schoolwork and extracurricular activities make it seem impossible to achieve a balance in life.

THE STRESS OF COVID-19

In early 2020, the COVID-19 pandemic began to spread across the world, transforming the daily lives of many Americans. Restrictions such as lockdowns and limits on gatherings were put into place. Many schools switched to remote learning. The sudden changes and sense of uncertainty about the future were disruptive and stressful for teens and parents alike.

The pandemic created and worsened many sources of stress for teens and deprived them of support systems, such as a regular routine of school activities and in-person interactions with friends. Many teens found it more difficult to learn remotely. Some saw a parent lose a job during the pandemic, causing financial strain. Family members also felt stressed, causing tensions when everybody was working or learning remotely from home. The CDC found that 55 percent of high school students experienced emotional abuse by an adult in their household, and 11 percent were physically abused. Rates were higher for LGBTQ+ teens.

As a result of the stresses of the pandemic era, many more teens reported experiencing mental health issues such as anxiety and depression. The isolation was particularly damaging to young people who were already struggling with mental illness.

The process of applying to colleges can be daunting, and many teens feel stressed about whether they'll be accepted into their top choice schools.

COLLEGE CONCERNS

Getting into college is a big deal for many teens, and it causes a lot of stress. Worrying about having the best application—and concern over how to pay for skyrocketing tuition—can be difficult for a teen to handle.

Sometimes teens put pressure on themselves regarding college and don't let their parents know what they're experiencing. College is a big and expensive life step. It's important, yes, but it won't decide everything about your life.

SCHOOL SHOOTINGS

School shootings are a big fear—and source of stress—for teens. More than 57 percent of teens say they are worried about a shooting happening at their school, according to a 2018 Pew Research Center study.

If you are scared about a school shooting, talk with an adult you trust, make a hotline call, or seek out a friend for some help. There are ways to stay safe, to understand the likelihood of something happening at your school, and to create positive change.

PEER PRESSURE

For some teens, having one or two good friends to hang out with is all they need to be comfortable. Others want to fit into and be accepted by a larger group. Regardless of how many people make up your peer group, their opinions are probably very important. Your friend group can have an incredible amount of influence on you. Decisions about whether or not to go along with the crowd will have to be made on many occasions. These decisions may be difficult and stressful to make.

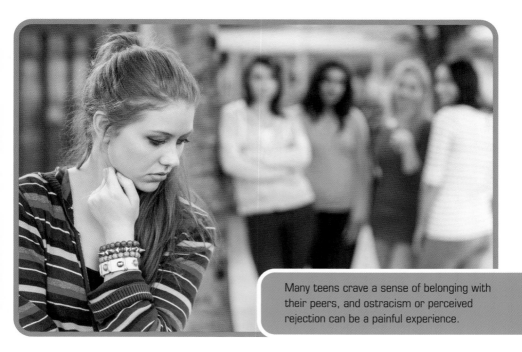

Many teens crave a sense of belonging with their peers, and ostracism or perceived rejection can be a painful experience.

DATING

It is not unusual for both members of a couple to be very busy with school, sports, and work. In this instance, they frequently feel that they have to "steal" time to be with each other. In some cases, one partner is busier than the other. The less busy partner feels that they come second place to everything else—a very stressful situation for both members of the couple.

Dating violence, defined as the intentional use of abusive tactics in order to obtain and maintain control over an intimate partner, can also be a major stressor for some teens. It should be reported to a responsible adult, but it can be difficult for victims to feel comfortable doing so. Victims often feel that they allowed the violence to happen so it is their own fault, or their abusers may have blamed them. Whatever the reason, if you are the victim of dating violence, you are not responsible. It is not your fault.

Because victims of date rape or dating violence have difficulty in taking steps to stop the violence, most communities have established hotlines. These are call centers that are manned 24/7 to provide initial help to those who need it. If you are a victim of dating violence, help is a phone call or a text away.

BULLYING

The term bullying is used to describe a variety of different behaviors, such as teasing, name-calling, intentionally not inviting someone to a social event, ignoring someone, or gossiping about them. At its extreme, bullying can also involve physical contact, like hitting, pinching, pushing, slapping, or other forms of assault.

As with dating violence, you need to let someone know if you are being bullied. When bullying occurs in schools, alerting a teacher or counselor would be a positive first step. Many schools have rules in place to try and deal with bullying. Hotlines are also available to provide help for those being bullied. Since many who are bullied become bullies, getting help early is important to avoid long-term problems.

A subtle form of bullying is social bullying, in which a bully undermines the victim's social standing through rumors, exclusion, or public humiliation.

In real life, most people don't look as flawless as the images of influencers, actors, and models seen on social media and television.

SELF-IMAGE

The way you perceive yourself may be closely tied to your peer group. It is not uncommon to want to be as attractive and outgoing as the most popular student in school. Remember that no one looks perfect all the time. Learning to live in your own skin is very hard to do, especially if you feel that your appearance is keeping you from being accepted by your peers. If you are having a difficult time accepting your appearance, consider talking with your parent or a doctor.

ONLINE STRESS

Any teen today will probably tell you that the internet is both terrible and wonderful. It's a great way to chat with friends, to follow musicians and actors, and to find out the answer to so many things. But the internet can also be a seriously stressful place.

CYBERBULLYING

Cyberbullying involves verbal harassment, rumor spreading, and the release of private information. About 46 percent of students reported being cyberbullied in 2021, according to the Cyberbullying Research Center. Many schools have anticyberbullying policies.

Cyberbullying can cause a great amount of stress. But there are things you can do to stop someone from bullying you online. Your first step may be to talk to a trusted adult, parent, teacher, or counselor.

Cyberbullying can occur at any time and place, and for the victim, the stress of the harassment can seem relentless.

SOCIAL MEDIA STRESS

How many likes did that picture get? Was everyone at that party but you? Social media can cause a lot of stress in a teen's life. There's fear of missing out (FOMO), in which it seems that everybody else is happier and having more fun. And teens can start to feel isolated when they spend too much time on social media rather than genuinely connecting with others. Excessive social media use has been linked with anxiety and depression.

One way to combat social media stress is to put down the phone. If you can limit your screen access, your feelings may improve.

MAKING A DIFFERENCE

The world can seem like a scary place. Worries about politics, the environment, the economy, and more can definitely stress a teen out. National and world issues are especially potent stressors because most teens feel there is nothing they can do about them. Not so! There is plenty a teen can do right now. Become active in groups working to combat racism, change gun laws, or protest climate change. Trying to cause positive change is a great way to relieve stress.

And remember, you're not alone. It might seem that nobody else understands the kind of stress you're experiencing. But your peers sometimes feel overwhelmed by responsibilities, expectations, and insecurities too, even if they don't show any signs of stress. Everybody finds their own ways to cope with stress.

Everybody feels stressed out at one time or another, so reach out to your friends when you're overwhelmed and be there for them when they need you.

CHAPTER 4

WHEN STRESS GETS OVERWHELMING

Stress can become so intolerable that people feel like they have to try to do something to relieve the pressure. There are healthy ways of dealing with stress. You might go for a run or turn to a friend for support. But some people respond with negative coping mechanisms in an attempt to push away the stress. These harmful ways of dealing with stress only cause more problems.

STAY AWAY FROM SUBSTANCES

Smoking, drinking, and drug use are examples of habits or behaviors that teens use to try to cope with the stressors in their lives. All of them have the potential to become addictions. Addiction is a condition in which your life is being controlled by some habit.

SMOKING

Nicotine is the addictive drug in tobacco that users need more and more of. The development of addiction to tobacco is a complex, learned process that involves actual physical changes in the body of the person as they experiment with tobacco use.

For many teens, smoking is a way of dealing with their stressful worlds. In the long run, however, it will only make things worse. And the teen years are when tobacco addiction typically takes hold. While most kids today are aware that smoking can lead to major health problems, there are still those who begin smoking—and it will be very difficult for them to stop.

Although nicotine is a very dangerous drug and is extremely addictive, its drug effect has been described as "mild." It doesn't take long for the body of a smoker to adapt to the drug, so smokers need to smoke more and more to get the same buzz they originally got with just a few cigarettes. Smoking is not a way to deal with stress. Instead, it will probably end up giving you more things to be stressed about in the future.

For smokers, their nicotine habit becomes integrated into their daily activities and may begin to control some aspects of those activities.

ALCOHOL ABUSE

Alcohol's large presence in American culture coupled with busy parents and rising rates of stress and depression among youths results in a "cocktail of reasons" explaining underage alcohol use. The stress of teen life, peer pressure, and a desire for independence contribute to teenage drinking.

The National Institute on Alcohol Abuse and Alcoholism reported that in 2019, more than 4.2 million teens participated in binge drinking (which means five or more drinks for males or four or more drinks for females within a few hours) in the past month. Binge drinking can lead to serious problems like increased risk of physical and sexual assault, injuries, and even death. The CDC reports that alcohol plays a role in 3,900 deaths of people 21 and under each year. The causes? Car accidents, alcohol poisoning, violence, and suicide.

The question is, does drinking alcohol really relieve stress? When an alcoholic beverage is consumed, alcohol gets into the bloodstream in a hurry. It takes about 30 minutes before the full effects of the drink are felt, but the brain gets its first jolt within 30 seconds. Most drinkers think that alcohol relieves stress because they initially feel good after taking a drink. But as with smoking, alcohol can cause more stress over time.

Alcohol is eliminated from the body much more slowly than it is absorbed. If you spend a full hour drinking a beer or sipping a glass of wine, you may never experience its effects because the alcohol is being eliminated about as rapidly as it is being consumed.

However, binge drinking means alcohol is being introduced into the system much more quickly.

In two weeks of drinking a couple of beers a day, the body and brain adapts to the alcohol. Then you have to increase your alcohol consumption considerably to get the reaction that you used to get with just two drinks. People who become addicted may experience withdrawal symptoms if they stop drinking. These symptoms can range from mild hand tremors, stomach upset, and excessive sweating to potentially life-threatening confusion, severe depression, hallucinations, and even seizures.

Like all addictive coping mechanisms, drinking alcohol does not relieve stress—it adds to your stress level.

It takes only three to four drinks within an hour for a man to be legally drunk, while a woman might be legally drunk with only two drinks in an hour.

DRUG ABUSE

A teen may use drugs to deal with life stress because of peer pressure or maybe even out of curiosity or boredom. Marijuana is the most commonly abused drug by teens, according to the 2021 Monitoring the Future survey.

Some teens might consider marijuana less dangerous than other drugs since it's widely used and legal in some states. But there is a larger concern for teen marijuana use, and it's that your brain isn't done developing yet. As the National Institute of Drug Abuse puts it, "The adolescent brain is often likened to a car with a fully functioning gas pedal (the reward system) but weak brakes (the prefrontal cortex)." Your brain will not be fully developed until your mid 20s. Marijuana use can harm the organ by making it harder to pay attention, remember things, and solve problems.

Many adults who wind up addicted to drugs begin using as teens. As a teen, your brain may be telling you to try out new experiences, but it is important to be mindful of the consequences of your decisions. If you're feeling stressed, will drug use help or cause more problems?

RISKY BEHAVIORS

People sometimes seek out distractions when they're stressed. Some are helpful, such as talking with a friend or going for a run. Others can be problematic, such as going shopping and getting into the habit of overspending. Turn the page to find some examples of unwise responses to stress.

LASHING OUT

People may respond to stress by lashing out at the people around them, even family and friends who are trying to help. Feelings of stress can cause anxiety, and anxiety is closely linked to anger. Both are natural responses to threatening situations. Anxiety and anger both produce some of the same physical symptoms, such as increased heart rate. People who are stressed can turn their anger on others, through irritable behavior or bursts of rage. It's an instinctive attempt to release tension.

Lashing out in anger might be a natural response, but it doesn't help reduce stress and it can damage relationships. Some of the same techniques used to manage stress, such as practicing healthy self-care and drawing on your support system, can also reduce feelings of anxiety and anger.

Some kids gamble for fun—and many of their gambling activities are actually innocent games played at parties with friends.

GAMBLING

Have you ever gambled? Sources of gambling are much more available now, thanks to online gambling, than it was in generations past.

Many teens start gambling to escape stress or because they can't say no to the temptation. But once a teen starts, they can get hooked—and then it is possible to become a compulsive gambler. Remember how your brain isn't done growing yet? A lot of stressed teens are significantly depressed and have very low self-esteem that gets boosted when they gamble and win. They find this boost gratifying. Unfortunately, they can get hooked on gambling, start to lose, and become more depressed and stressed.

SEX

Most teens will face the question of whether or not to become sexually active and when. For some, there may be conflicts between what one has been brought up to believe about sexual relationships and what one is being encouraged to do by potential sexual partners. This can create a tremendous amount of stress. Teens who are consciously deciding about becoming sexually active should think things through, choose a caring partner, and always use protection.

Sexual assault is also a very serious stressor. According to RAINN, the Rape, Abuse & Incest National Network, women ages 16 to 19 are four times more likely than the rest of the general population to be the victim of rape, attempted rape, or sexual assault. You have the right to say no to having sex at any time, even if you have said yes before. And if someone says no to you during a sexual encounter, you must stop immediately.

Some of these unhealthy reactions to stress can lead to lifelong consequences. It's important for teens to develop healthy coping skills early on for dealing with stress and other negative situations. This will equip you with the positivity and resilience to maintain a sense of balance despite the small annoyances and major traumas of life.

Sexual abuse can have serious consequences for one's life and mental health, including an increased likelihood of abusing drugs, and experiencing PTSD and depression.

CHAPTER 5

MANAGING STRESS

As you've seen, stress is a pressing issue for teens that can have serious consequences. And it's important to avoid responding with destructive behaviors that will only cause more problems. Fortunately, there are a number of healthy strategies that can help you manage the sources of stress in your life.

Two common approaches for dealing with stress are problem-based and emotion-based coping tactics. When you use problem-based coping, you tackle the root cause of the source of stress. You might achieve this by working to change the situation, managing your time, or asking for help. When you use emotion-based coping, you adjust your own feelings toward the source of stress. This approach may be more successful in situations beyond your control, whether it's something small like your bus running late or a major life event, such as grieving over the death of a loved one.

Everybody develops their own coping strategies based on what works best for them. But if you're having trouble managing stress, you should consider taking a step back and asking if a different approach might be more effective.

BUILDING SELF-ESTEEM

Self-image is the way you see yourself in relation to others. Improving your self-image is the first step in having a positive "sense of self." It's also important to develop healthy self-esteem. Self-esteem is the opinion you have of yourself. This includes your value as a person, your achievements, your purpose in life, your strengths and weaknesses, and your independence.

FEELING BETTER ABOUT YOURSELF

So how do you improve your self-image and boost your self-esteem? One possible first step to improving self-image is to list things you like about yourself. As you do that, you will undoubtedly think of things you do not like about yourself. Ask whether you are being too hard on yourself. If you decide to improve your self-image, start with easy ones such as changing your hair or getting a few new clothes. Take a positive approach to things that are harder to change, like your weight. Think of them as challenges instead of obstacles.

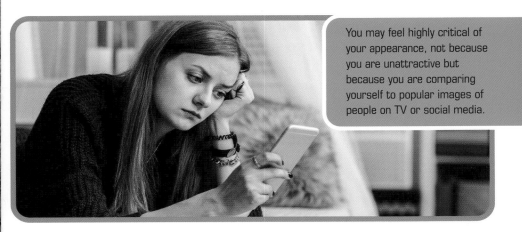

You may feel highly critical of your appearance, not because you are unattractive but because you are comparing yourself to popular images of people on TV or social media.

USE POSITIVE SPEECH

If you stop to think about it, you are constantly having mental conversations with yourself. If you bad-mouth yourself in these conversations, you may soon believe you are a bad person. Put a positive spin on your mental conversations rather than a negative one. For instance, if you have done badly on a test at school, instead of saying to yourself, "You dummy, how could you be so stupid?" think, "Wow, that was a hard test. I really need to study harder for the next one."

Be tolerant of your own mistakes. Nobody is perfect. It is easy to be excessively critical of yourself, especially when things are not going well. Mistakes happen, but the key is to admit when you make one, learn from it, then let it go.

ACKNOWLEDGE YOUR ACCOMPLISHMENTS

Most teens feel that passing their driver's license test or getting really high grades is a big accomplishment, but you should also recognize your smaller accomplishments. Getting to school on time or receiving a compliment at work are also things that should matter. Make a daily list of those things, even if they don't seem very important. By recognizing your accomplishments, you begin to understand that you have self-worth.

BE ASSERTIVE

Being able to let others know what you think and feel is important. After all, what you have to say is just as important as what others have to say. As a teen, you may think your parents and other adults do not want to know what you think or what is important to you, but most adults welcome conversations with teens. Say what you think, but also listen to others and respect their opinions.

Spend time with people who value you. Listen to what they say about you. People you choose to be around are often mirrors of how you feel about yourself. If others are constantly putting you down, you're running with the wrong crowd!

Spending time with friends can help relieve stress, whether you're getting together to provide mutual support or just going out to have fun.

Once you've identified the major sources of stress in your everyday life, you can formulate a plan to deal with them.

TAKING CONTROL

With your self-image buffed and your self-esteem maximized, you are ready to deal with stress and make it work for you. Here are a few steps that will help you to take control.

DEFINE THE PROBLEM

Know that you cannot eliminate all stress from your life. Who can? Define your individual list of major stressors. Take the time to analyze your day. Write down how you spent your time, who you interacted with, and how you responded to situations. It is especially important to note your feelings—were you happy, sad, or infuriated? Keep track of these things for several days, then set aside an hour or so to analyze your notes. You may be surprised to find out what did or did not cause you stress.

LEARN TO MANAGE YOUR TIME

One of the main stressors identified by teens is the lack of time to do everything that is expected of them. You're being pulled in a million different directions—school, work, extracurricular activities, friends, family—it's exhausting just thinking about it! But if you exercise good time management and work to schedule activities you have to do, as well as those you want to do, it can help you keep control of your schedule.

List those daily and weekly activities that you know you have to do. Always list your routine commitments, like classes, band practice, student council meetings, or after-school jobs. After you get all of the "must-dos" into your schedule, start filling in uncommitted time slots with things you should do, like getting a head start on research for a term paper or volunteering to help with your kid brother's school carnival. You are in control of this schedule, so build time into it for everything: alone time, family time, recreational time, or even time to sleep.

Realistically, no schedule will ever be perfect. Your friends will still call to chat or want you to go out at inopportune times, and occasionally you will rebel against the regimentation you are imposing on yourself. But that's OK. You'll be more likely to stick to your schedule if you allow yourself some leeway.

If you keep to your schedule most of the time, you will find even an incredibly taxing workload to be much less stressful than it was before.

HOW TO SAY NO

One major source of stress is agreeing to too many commitments. It can be hard to refuse when somebody makes a request or proposal. You might feel guilty about saying no or you may worry that they'll be upset. Maybe you tell yourself that you can manage one more commitment, even though you're feeling stressed and exhausted. But it's important to learn to say no to people. Taking on too many responsibilities might mean that you won't perform as well at any of them. You need to learn to establish boundaries, set priorities, and learn to manage your time, which includes allowing yourself personal time for relaxing and self-care. And remember, you don't owe anyone an explanation or apology when you say no to them. Simply tell them firmly and politely that you're not able to do it or that you already have plans. If you're undecided, say that you'll think it over or suggest a slightly smaller commitment that you can manage. Learning to balance your options will reduce stress and allow you to fully commit to the priorities that are most important to you.

PRACTICE AND PREPARE

One of the most stressful things you can do is approach an event without preparation. For example, perhaps you're required to give a brief talk in front of your history class. You know the material well, but the thought of presenting it puts you in a panic. Practice your talk in front of a mirror beforehand. Give the talk to your parents, a friend, or even your dog. You will find that because you have practiced and are prepared, you have harnessed your stress and made it work for you. When the time comes to present your subject, you will be more relaxed than if you had not prepared.

FINISH WHAT YOU START

With your busy schedule, you may find that you never quite finish anything to your satisfaction. Projects or chores that you started weeks ago are still hanging over your head while you try to deal with more urgent matters. Eventually, everything piles up and you may begin to feel overwhelmed. You can minimize stress by making a concerted effort to finish each project or chore as it comes along. Break big projects into a group of smaller tasks that can be completed in a reasonable amount of time. You will get a great deal of satisfaction from actually finishing something you've started.

PRACTICING SELF-CARE

Coping with outside stressors if you are physically stressed is very difficult. These are the "big three" of staying physically healthy:

Eat right and stay hydrated. Stress reactions require your body to expend tremendous amounts of energy. You get the fuel for these reactions from food, but grabbing a quick bite when you're busy could mean you're eating a lot of fast food, snacks, and sodas. These foods are high in calories, fats, and caffeine, and they're low in basic nutrients, vitamins, and minerals. Your body isn't getting what it needs to help you fuel your

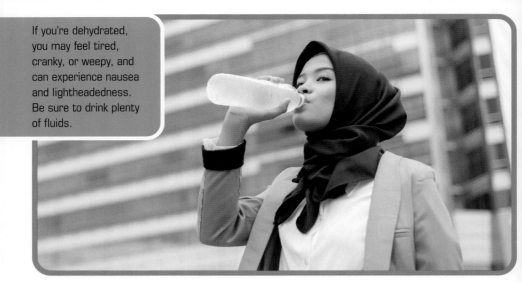

If you're dehydrated, you may feel tired, cranky, or weepy, and can experience nausea and lightheadedness. Be sure to drink plenty of fluids.

stress reactions, and it's being overwhelmed with things that may worsen these reactions, so take the time to eat well-rounded meals. Your body also needs water to keep all your systems working.

Get enough sleep. Sleep deprivation problems can add to the stressors in your life. People usually need seven or eight hours of sleep a night, but most teens don't get that much. Melatonin, a hormone that regulates sleeping and waking patterns, is produced later at night in teens than it is in younger kids and adults. Teens tend to fall asleep later at night and, if their schedules allow, sleep later in the morning. However, teens who fall asleep after midnight may still have to be up early for school, so over time they may become sleep deprived.

Get plenty of exercise. Exercise has three major benefits in helping to control stress. First, it helps to counterbalance the added caloric intake that is common in kids on the run. By expending some of those extra calories in physical activity, teens are less likely to gain weight and will have an easier time maintaining a positive self-image. Second of all, exercise can decrease stress by causing increased production of endorphins, or natural opioids, in the brain. This gives a natural high that counterbalances the lows of stress. The third benefit of exercise is that you'll have an outlet for all the pent-up energy that stress produces.

Many of these approaches toward handling stress help build up your resilience in dealing with difficult circumstances. If you're resilient, you'll be able to adapt when faced with challenges. Depending on what you think best for the situation, you might opt to make a plan, use your strengths to their best advantage, work with others on a solution, or manage your perspective on the situation. Developing resilience takes time, and with every success, you'll gain confidence that will help you handle stress in the future.

Sleep deprivation can lead to impairment in judgment and the ability to think, as well as impairment of motor skills and reaction times.

CHAPTER 6

SEEKING HELP

Connecting with others is an important aspect of managing stress. You'll cope better if you're willing to ask for help when you need it, on matters large and small. You'll feel better about your situation if you have a strong support system of family and friends. Don't make the mistake of isolating yourself or withdrawing from others when you're feeling stressed. It can be hard to admit that you need help, but reaching out to others when you're in difficult circumstances is a sign of strength, not weakness.

Try asking yourself these questions before reaching out to someone:

- Why do I think I need help?
- How severe are my stressors?
- Are my stressors day-to-day problems, like trying to manage time or meeting obligations?
- Are my stressors bigger things, such as trying to cope with life transitions or peer pressure?
- Are my stressors truly traumatic, like being hooked on drugs?
- What kind of help do I need?

By clarifying the answers to these questions, you will be more likely to ask the right person for help. You will also be able to express your needs more clearly when you do ask for help.

REACHING OUT

Once you have decided that you need help, the challenge is to reach out and talk to someone. Who will listen and not be judgmental? Who can help? Care and support may be found among friends and family. If you seek an ear outside of your circle, school counselors, therapists, and support groups can be great resources.

Ask your high school counselor or family doctor about where you could find a support group if you're feeling stressed.

It's normal to clash with parents as you're growing up and establishing your own identity, but they're there to offer guidance and support when you need it.

PARENTS

Those of you who can comfortably talk to your parents are truly lucky. You know that you can bring even the most stressful situation to them and be assured of getting sound advice. However, teens can also be stressed by conflicts with their parents. And the inability to communicate with a parent can also create conflicts.

The very fact that you are maturing may be one of the prime problems. As you are gaining confidence in yourself and your ability to resolve problems, your parents are having a hard time realizing that you aren't the little kid they have been making decisions for all these years. The

disparity between how you see yourself and how your parents see you can lead to disagreements. In some cases, you may decide that you simply can't talk with them, and they may decide the same thing.

When you run into stressors that you can't handle alone, in spite of your new maturity, it is frequently hard to reopen lines of communication with your parents. Try defining the issues you want to discuss with your parents. You may find it helpful to actually write down the most important points you want to cover so you don't forget them. Limit these to three or four main topics. Be clear that you have an important issue you want to discuss. Schedule your talk for a specific time when you will have their undivided attention. Finally, write down your thoughts and give them to your parents before the discussion.

FAMILY AND FRIENDS

You can also reach out to other adults available in your life. Consider, do you have a favorite teacher, coach, member of a religious group, grandparent, aunt, or uncle who can listen and provide comfort? They can also know when to steer you to a professional who can help.

You may even turn to your friends. Real friends are those who will tell you what you need to hear, not what you want to hear. If you are scared, depressed, confused, or desperate to escape from a situation or habit that has gotten out of hand, choose a friend you trust who will be brutally honest with you and talk to that person. This friend may already know a lot about what you are feeling.

SUPPORT GROUPS

One of the most effective ways of dealing with a problem is to meet with other people who have experienced or are experiencing the same thing. There are support groups for people dealing with mental or physical illness, grief, or substance abuse issues. Support groups also exist for members of marginalized groups and victims of violence or trauma. In some communities, you may be able to find a support group specifically for stressed teenagers. Support groups may be affiliated with a health care provider or a non-profit organization. The main advantage of this type of group lies in knowing that others understand the problems you are having because they've all been there. You can find support groups online. Many have hotlines or online chat options that you can use if you feel desperate. They honestly care and can help you deal with a crisis, as well as continue to provide support as long as you need it.

School guidance counselors are knowledgeable about the availability of support groups or therapists they can refer you to should you need it.

A therapist can help teens learn about themselves, discover ways to overcome troubling feelings and behaviors, and develop good coping skills.

COUNSELORS AND PSYCHOTHERAPISTS

A school counselor's job is to help kids cope with problems. They have special training in many areas, so they aren't limited to helping with school issues.

Sometimes a teen will have problems so troubling that friends and/or parents feel unable to give the teen adequate help. At that point, the teen may have to see a psychotherapist. A therapist is professionally trained to help with emotional and behavioral problems.

The approach a therapist uses depends on a teen's individual needs, but it always includes listening, exchanging information, building trust, and respecting confidentiality. In some instances, a therapist may recommend and prescribe medication to help a teen through a crisis. Few require long-term drug therapy. Once a teen and their therapist have developed a workable plan for dealing with stressors, it will be up to the teen to implement the plan with the therapist's help.

If you cultivate good habits for managing stress as a teen, you'll be in good shape for taking on adult responsibilities later on in life.

The teen years can be a time of major life crises. You are experiencing many physical changes that can be stressful. You are developing your own beliefs and values. You are faced with the challenges of deciding your future educational goals, where to take relationships, and how to respond to endless demands on your time. You are also living in an era of unprecedented technological expansion that is mind-boggling. Is there any wonder that you are stressed?

As you have seen, there are many ways to cope with stress. Don't ignore the consequences of stress in your life—stress won't go away on its own. By learning about how stress works and about the various healthy approaches to managing stress, you can take control and tame the sources of stress in your life. You can address your stress by cultivating resilience and positivity, managing your time wisely, practicing self-care, connecting with others, and maintaining a healthy self-image. Many of the skills that you utilize in dealing with stress can help you succeed in other areas throughout your life.

10 GREAT QUESTIONS TO ASK A DOCTOR ABOUT STRESS

1. Could my stress contribute to physical or mental health conditions?

2. Could lifestyle changes, such as diet or exercise, help reduce the stress I'm feeling?

3. How can I develop a positive attitude toward challenges?

4. What activities or self-care practices can help me when I'm feeling stressed?

5. How can better time management strategies help me deal with stress?

6. What substances should I stay away from if I feel really stressed?

7. Are there any programs to help students manage stress?

8. Are there any books, DVDs, or websites that could help me learn about my symptoms?

9. Are there any support groups, mental health providers, or non-profit organizations in my community where I can go for help?

10. How do I find a therapist who can help me handle stress?

Your family doctor can evaluate any physical and mental symptoms of stress you're experiencing and recommend strategies for reducing and managing stress.

adrenaline: A hormone made in the adrenal glands in response to stress.

adrenocorticotropic hormone (ACTH): Produced by the pituitary gland, ACTH instructs the adrenal glands to produce cortisol.

antidepressant: A medication used to relieve depression and sometimes anxiety disorders.

anxiety: An emotion characterized by feelings of tension, worried thoughts, and physical changes like increased blood pressure.

autonomic nervous system: Also known as the involuntary nervous system, it controls the body's ability to relax and digest and is in charge of the flight-or-flight response.

corticotropin-releasing hormone (CRH): Made by the hypothalamus in response to stress, CRH tells the pituitary gland to make ACTH.

cortisol: The main stress hormone, cortisol increases glucose in the bloodstream and helps with the fight-or-flight response, among other things.

depression: A mental illness that causes feelings of sadness, hopelessness, and despair.

endorphins: Chemicals produced in the brain that can cause euphoria or other positive feelings.

gambling: To play a game for money or other stakes.

glucose: A simple sugar that is the main energy source for body reactions. Many glucose molecules are combined and stored in the liver and other tissues as glycogen. When needed, glycogen is broken down into smaller glucose molecules.

herpes simplex virus (HSV): The virus that causes herpes and sometimes causes small blisters on the mouth and lips, also called cold sores.

hormone: A chemical substance produced in one place in the body that is carried through the bloodstream to another part of the body where it causes some type of reaction.

hypothalamus: The region of the brain that controls the autonomic nervous system by regulating functions such as sleep cycles, appetite, and body temperature.

physiology: The study of the function of the organs and other body parts during life.

platelet: A tiny, colorless, disc-shaped structure found in blood that, when disrupted, initiates the clotting of blood.

post-traumatic stress disorder (PTSD): A disorder, often marked by flashbacks and severe anxiety, that develops after a traumatic experience.

stressor: A stimulus that causes the stress response.

syndrome: A group of signs and symptoms that occur together and characterize a disease or disorder.

AMERICAN INSTITUTE OF STRESS (AIS)
220 Adams Drive
Suite 280 #224
Weatherford, TX 76086 USA
(682) 239-6823
Email: *info@stress.org*
Website: *www.stress.org*
Facebook: *@aistress*
Twitter: *@AIS_StressNews*
The AIS provides medical professionals and the public with information about stress and conducts research on stress.

CANADIAN MENTAL HEALTH ASSOCIATION
250 Dundas Street West, Suite 500
Toronto, ON M5T 2Z5
Canada
(416) 646-5557
Email: *info@cmha.ca*
Website: *www.cmha.ca*
Facebook: *@CMHA.ACSM.National*
Instagram: *@cmhanational*
Twitter: *@CMHA_NTL*
CMHA provides mental health programs and services to Canadians and advocates for mental health care for all Canadians.

CENTERS FOR DISEASE CONTROL AND PREVENTION (CDC)

1600 Clifton Road
Atlanta, GA 30329-4027
(800) 232-4636
Website: *www.cdc.gov/*
Facebook: *@cdc*
Instagram and Twitter: *@CDCgov*
Part of the U.S. Department of Health & Human Services, the CDC is charged with protecting the health of all Americans. Its site includes information, help, and resources on dealing with stress, including tools for teens.

THE JED FOUNDATION

530 7th Avenue, Suite 801
New York, NY 10018
(212) 647-7544
Website: *jedfoundation.org*
Facebook, Instagram, Twitter: *@JedFoundation*
The Jed Foundation provides resources for emotional support, including managing stress, and suicide prevention for young adults.

PSYCHOLOGY TODAY

115 E. 23rd St., 9th Floor
New York, NY 10010
Website: *www.psychologytoday.com/*
Facebook: *@psychologytoday*
Instagram: *@psych_today*
Twitter: *@psychtoday*
Psychology Today is a magazine and online site focusing on psychology and mental health. It provides listings for mental health professionals as well as resources on mental health issues.

SUBSTANCE ABUSE AND MENTAL HEALTH SERVICES ADMINISTRATION (SAMHSA)

5600 Fishers Lane
Rockville, MD 20857
(877) 726-4727
Website: *www.samhsa.gov/*
Facebook: *@samhsa*
Instagram, Twitter: *@samhsagov*
Part of the U.S. Department of Health and Human Services, SAMHSA works to promote mental health, prevent substance misuse, and provide treatment and support to people with mental health or substance abuse issues.

TEEN LINE

Cedars-Sinai
PO Box 48750
Los Angeles, CA 90048
(800) 852-8336
Email: *admin@teenlineonline.org*
Website: *www.teenline.org*
Facebook, Instagram, Twitter: *@teenlineonline*
The Teen Line helpline offers mental health support
provided by trained teen counselors.

Benson, Kerry Elizabeth. *Everything You Need to Know About Mindfulness*. Buffalo, NY: Rosen Publishing, 2020.

Bernstein, Jeffrey. *Mindfulness for Teen Worry: Quick & Easy Strategies to Let Go of Anxiety, Worry, & Stress*. Oakland, CA: Instant Help Publications, 2017.

George, Mike. *You Can Relax and Avoid Stress*. New York, NY: Rosen Publishing, 2018.

Harts, Shannon H. *Stress and Anxiety*. Buffalo, NY: Rosen Publishing, 2021.

Hugstad, Kristi. *Be You, Only Better: Real Life Self-Care for Young Adults (and Everyone Else)*. Novato, CA: New World Library, 2021.

Landau, Jennifer. *Teens Talk About Self-Esteem and Self-Confidence*. New York, NY: Rosen Publishing, 2018.

Parys, Sabrina. *Everything You Need to Know About Stress and Depression*. New York, NY: Rosen Publishing, 2018.

Scientific American Editors. *Stressed Out: Causes, Effects & Keeping Calm.* Buffalo, NY: Rosen Publishing, 2020.

Skeen, Michelle. *Just as You Are: A Teen's Guide to Self-Acceptance and Lasting Self-Esteem.* Oakland, CA: New Harbinger Publications, Inc., 2018.

Thomas, Bonnie. *Creative Self-Care and Coping Skills for Teens and Tweens: Emotional Support Through Art, Yoga, Mindfulness and More.* Philadelphia, PA: Jessica Kingsley Publishers, 2019.

A

abuse, 19–20, 25, 31, 34, 47
addiction, 40–44
alcohol, 40, 42–43
American Heart Association, 17
American Psychological Association (APA), 23
antidepressants, 20
anxiety, 21–23, 25, 31, 38, 45

B

bullying, 34–35, 37

C

Cannon, Walter Bradford, 4–5
Centers for Disease Control and Prevention (CDC), 18, 25, 31
college, 4, 24, 27, 29, 30, 32
counselors, 26, 28, 30, 35, 58–59, 62, 63
COVID-19, 31
cyberbullying, 37

D

dating, 34
depression, 20–22, 25, 31, 38, 42–43, 46–47
diet, 55–56, 66
divorce, 26
drugs, 40, 44, 58

E

exercise, 56–57, 66

F

fight-or-flight response, 5

G

gambling, 46
gastrointestinal problems, 16–17
general adaptation syndrome (GAS), 10–11
grades, 27, 29–30, 50
grief, 26, 48, 62

H

heart attack, 6, 17
herpes simplex virus (HSV), 15
hormones, 5, 7, 9–10, 14–19, 21–23, 56
hypertension, 17, 21

I

immune system, 14–16

L

LGBTQ+, 31

O

obesity, 18

P

panic attacks, 22
post-traumatic stress disorder (PTSD), 20, 47

S

school shootings, 32–33
self-care, 54–57, 65, 66
Selye, Hans, 4–6, 10–11
sex, 46–47
sex hormones, 18
sleep, 56–57
smoking, 40–41
social media, 14, 23–24, 36, 38, 49
stress reactions, 6–10, 15, 55
stroke, 6, 17
suicide, 21–22, 42
support groups, 59, 62

T

therapy, 63–66
time management, 52–53, 58

V

violence, 32–35, 42, 47, 62

ABOUT THE AUTHOR

ALEX NOVAK is a freelance writer who has written many nonfiction books for children and teens. Many of them address issues teenagers face in their daily lives, including *Hate and Intolerance* (Coping). She lives in New York.

PHOTO CREDITS